OSTRICH VS. CHEETAH

BY NATHAN SOMMER

BELLWETHER MEDIA • MINNEAPOLIS, MN

Torque brims with excitement
perfect for thrill-seekers of all kinds.
Discover daring survival skills, explore
uncharted worlds, and marvel at mighty
engines and extreme sports. In *Torque* books,
anything can happen. Are you ready?

Library of Congress Cataloging-in-Publication Data

Names: Sommer, Nathan, author.
Title: Ostrich vs. cheetah / by Nathan Sommer.
Other titles: Ostrich versus cheetah
Description: Minneapolis, MN : Bellwether Media, Inc., 2023. | Series:
    Animal battles | Includes bibliographical references and index. |
    Audience: Ages 7-12 | Audience: Grades 4-6 | Summary: "Amazing
    photography accompanies engaging information about the fighting
    advantages of ostriches and cheetahs. The combination of high-interest
    subject matter and light text is intended for students in grades 3
    through 7"– Provided by publisher.
Identifiers: LCCN 2022038231 (print) | LCCN 2022038232 (ebook) | ISBN
    9798886871661 (library binding) | ISBN 9798886872149 (paperback) | ISBN
    9798886872927 (ebook)
Subjects: LCSH: Ostriches–Juvenile literature. | Cheetah–Juvenile
    literature.
Classification: LCC QL696.S9 S63 2023 (print) | LCC QL696.S9 (ebook) |
    DDC 598.5/24–dc23/eng/20220829
LC record available at https://lccn.loc.gov/2022038231
LC ebook record available at https://lccn.loc.gov/2022038232

Editor: Kieran Downs   Designer: Josh Brink

Printed in the United States of America, North Mankato, MN.

TABLE OF CONTENTS

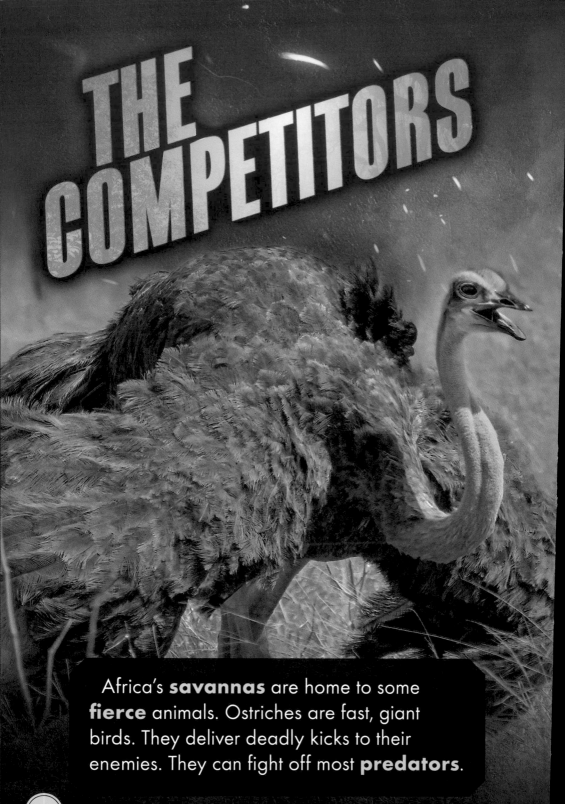

THE COMPETITORS

Africa's **savannas** are home to some **fierce** animals. Ostriches are fast, giant birds. They deliver deadly kicks to their enemies. They can fight off most **predators**.

But speedy cheetahs are on the hunt. Few can escape these big cats when they are hungry. Who wins when these beasts face off?

Ostriches are the world's largest birds. They stand up to 9 feet (2.7 meters) tall and weigh up to 350 pounds (159 kilograms). The birds have long necks, strong legs, and soft feathers.

Ostriches are found in Africa's savannas and deserts. They mostly eat plants and bugs. Ostriches live in **herds**. Most herds include around 12 birds.

HERD

THE LARGEST EGGS

Ostriches lay the largest eggs in the world. Some eggs can weigh up to 3 pounds (1.4 kilograms)!

OSTRICH PROFILE

10 FEET

8 FEET

WEIGHT
UP TO 350 POUNDS
(159 KILOGRAMS)

6 FEET

4 FEET

HEIGHT
UP TO 9 FEET
(2.7 METERS)

2 FEET

0

HABITAT

SAVANNAS

DESERTS

OSTRICH RANGE

☐ RANGE

CHEETAH PROFILE

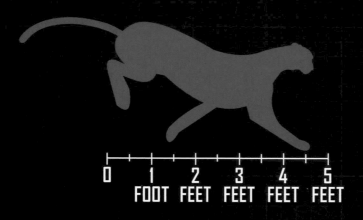

```
0        1       2       3       4       5
FOOT    FEET    FEET    FEET    FEET    FEET
```

LENGTH
UP TO 4.6 FEET
(1.4 METERS)

WEIGHT
UP TO 143 POUNDS
(64.9 KILOGRAMS)

HABITAT

SAVANNAS   DESERTS

CHEETAH RANGE

 RANGE

Cheetahs are the world's fastest land animals. These big cats have thin bodies, black spots, and long tails.

Cheetahs live in savannas and deserts in Africa and Iran. They mostly hunt birds and small animals like rabbits and young antelopes. Males live and hunt in groups of two or three. Females usually live alone.

SECRET WEAPONS

Ostriches have great eyesight. Their large eyes spot predators from far away. They warn other ostriches to run away.

Cheetahs use their spots to blend into their **habitats**. The spots help them match shadows in the grass. This allows them to easily sneak up on **prey**.

Ostriches are flightless. Instead, they run at speeds of up to 45 miles (72.4 kilometers) per hour. Their long legs can cover up to 16 feet (4.9 meters) in one step!

70 MILES
(112.6 KILOMETERS)
PER HOUR

CHEETAH

45 MILES
(72.4 KILOMETERS)
PER HOUR

OSTRICH

28 MILES
(45 KILOMETERS)
PER HOUR

HUMAN

Cheetahs are even faster than ostriches.
They **sprint** at speeds of around 70 miles
(112.6 kilometers) per hour. **Adapted** paw pads
and long tails keep them balanced at high speeds.

SECRET WEAPONS

EYESIGHT

SPEED

POWERFUL LEGS

TOE CLAWS

Ostriches kick enemies that come too close. Their powerful legs and sharp toe claws cause a lot of damage. One kick is enough to kill a lion!

CHEETAH

BLACK SPOTS

SPEED

SEMI-RETRACTABLE CLAWS

Cheetahs have **semi-retractable claws**. They help the cats grab the ground when running. These sharp claws are also used to **slash** and hurt prey.

ATTACK MOVES

Ostriches flop on the ground when danger is nearby. They lay their heads and necks flat to blend in with the sand. They quickly run away if spotted.

Cheetahs **stalk** their prey. When they get close enough, they use their speed to attack! Their sharp claws easily grab hold of most prey.

UNBELIEVABLE SPEED

Cheetahs can go from 0 to 60 miles (97 kilometers) per hour in just 3 seconds. Many cars cannot do that!

Ostriches fight when they cannot escape. They use their powerful legs to kick enemies. They slash with their claws. Then they stomp the bodies of attackers.

TWO-TOED

Ostriches are the only birds that have two toes. All other birds have at least three toes.

BUILT FOR SPEED

Cheetahs have large lungs. These allow the cats to take in more air as they run at high speeds.

Cheetahs take down small prey with one bite to the head or neck. Larger prey is **suffocated** by cheetahs' strong jaws. The cats eat quickly so their meal is not stolen!

A cheetah hides in tall grass. It watches an ostrich wander from its herd. The cat creeps closer. But the ostrich spots it. The chase is on!

The cheetah closes in on the ostrich. But the bird delivers a crushing kick. The wounded cheetah runs off. It is no match for the ostrich's powerful legs!

GLOSSARY

adapted—changed over a long period of time

fierce—strong and intense

habitats—the homes or areas where animals prefer to live

herds—groups of ostriches

predators—animals that hunt other animals for food

prey—animals that are hunted by other animals for food

savannas—flat grasslands in Africa with very few trees

semi-retractable claws—claws that are out and visible at all times

slash—to cut with a sharp object

sprint—to run at full speed for a short distance

stalk—to follow closely and quietly

suffocated—stopped from breathing

TO LEARN MORE

AT THE LIBRARY

Emminizer, Theresa. *Awesome Ostriches*. New York, N.Y.:
PowerKids Press, 2021.

Murray, Julie. *Cheetahs*. Minneapolis, Minn.:
Abdo Publishing, 2020.

Rossiter, Brienna. *World's Fastest Animals*. Lake Elmo, Minn.:
Apex, 2022.

ON THE WEB

FACTSURFER

Factsurfer.com gives you
a safe, fun way to find
more information.

1. Go to www.factsurfer.com

2. Enter "ostrich vs. cheetah " into the search box
   and click 🔍.

3. Select your book cover to see a list of related content.

INDEX